Teddy Roosevelt
The People's President

written by **Sharon Gayle**

illustrated by **Bob Dacey**
and Debra Bandelin

Aladdin

New York   London   Toronto   Sydney   Singapore

To my best friend, Denise:
Thank you. —S. G.

To Joe "T. R." Glisson with appreciation. —B. D. and D. B.

First Aladdin Paperbacks edition January 2004

Text copyright © 2004 by Sharon Gayle
Illustrations copyright © 2004 by Bob Dacey and Debra Bandelin

ALADDIN PAPERBACKS
An imprint of Simon & Schuster Children's Publishing Division
1230 Avenue of the Americas
New York, NY 10020

Book design by Lisa Vega
The text of this book was set in Century Old Style.

Printed in the United States of America
2 4 6 8 10 9 7 5 3 1

Library of Congress Cataloging-in-Publication Data

Gayle, Sharon.
Teddy Roosevelt : the people's president / by Sharon Gayle ;
illustrated by Bob Dacey and Debra Bandelin.—1st Aladdin Paperbacks ed.
p. cm. — (Ready-to-read stories of famous Americans)
Summary: Profiles the life of the Theodore Roosevelt, from his sickly childhood, which he
overcame to become a robust outdoorsman, leader of the Rough Riders and later, the twenty-
sixth president of the United States.
ISBN 0-689-85825-6 (pbk.) — ISBN 0-689-85826-4 (library edition)
1. Roosevelt, Theodore, 1858–1919—Juvenile literature. 2. Presidents—United States—
Biography—Juvenile literature. [1. Roosevelt, Theodore, 1858–1919. 2. Presidents.]
I. Dacey, Bob, ill. II. Bandelin, Debra, ill. III. Title. IV. Series.
E757.G39 2004
973.91'1'092—dc21   2003007530

Teddy Roosevelt
The People's President

Chapter 1
Fearless!

"Charge!" cried Commander Theodore Roosevelt as he led his soldiers up the mountainside. It was July 1898. The commander and his men were in the mountains of Cuba. The air was hot and sticky. They were surrounded by snakes and insects. But the commander and his men did not mind. They were strong and sure of themselves.

But Teddy Roosevelt, as he was known, was not always so strong. Theodore Roosevelt, the second of four children, was born in New York City on October 27, 1858. Named after his father, Teddy was a weak little baby and suffered from poor health all through his childhood. He had very bad asthma and often had to be rushed to the hospital. But Teddy's parents always believed that one day he would become strong and healthy.

Even though he found it hard to breathe, Teddy loved to play. One day he realized he couldn't see things far away. His parents took him to many eye doctors. All of the doctors said the same thing. Teddy was nearsighted and had to wear glasses. Teddy was very upset about this. But he wore his eyeglasses everyday for the rest of his life, and the round silver glasses became his trademark.

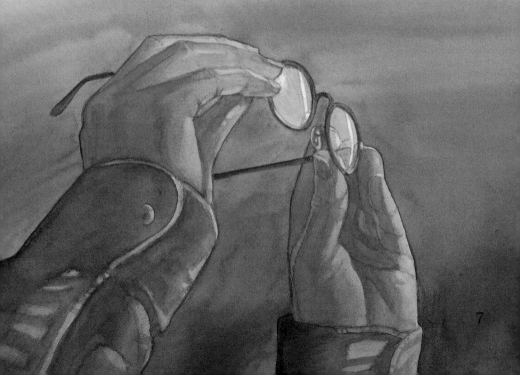

When Teddy was twelve, his father decided that Teddy might get stronger if he lived outdoors. He sent Teddy to Maine for a long camping trip. A servant went with him.

While camping, young Theodore was bothered by two local boys. They tormented him. Teddy was ashamed because he was too weak to fight the boys. From then on he decided to build his body so he could fight back.

Young Theodore also loved books and the outdoors. He loved to study nature. Teddy's room was filled with mice and birds and leaves. His mother, Mittie, writes of him coming in the house covered with mud. But the Roosevelts didn't care.

Around the same time, Teddy's father built a gym so Teddy could exercise every day. Teddy grew strong and healthy. He even overcame his asthma. Teddy also became the most fearless boy in his neighborhood. He never turned down the chance to fight bullies wherever he went.

At the age of eighteen Teddy went to Harvard University and became an honor student. No longer weak and sickly, Teddy was a strong, healthy, and smart young man.

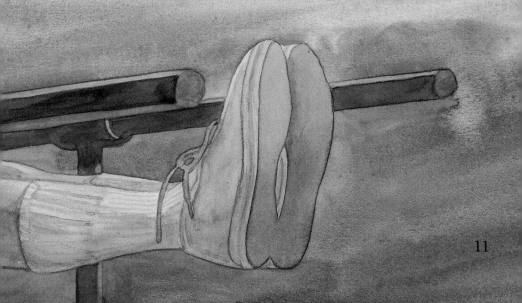

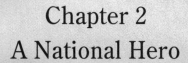

Chapter 2
A National Hero

Little did Teddy know that the lessons he learned as a child would help him when he grew up.

In 1884 double tragedy struck. Teddy's wife, Alice Roosevelt, died two days after the birth of their daughter, also named Alice. On the very same day Teddy's mother, Martha Bulloch Roosevelt, died of typhoid fever.

It was a hard time for Teddy. He decided to go out West. There he ran two cattle ranches. Teddy was most happy during this time when he was outdoors with the wind in his face. Riding his horse for fourteen to sixteen hours a day helped Teddy forget his loss. He hunted buffalo and wild animals. Once he even helped a local sheriff capture a band of outlaws.

But once again bad times came for Teddy. Terrible snowstorms during the winter of 1885 to 1886 killed most of his cattle. He decided that ranching was not for him and returned to New York City.

When Teddy left the West, he married his second wife Edith Kermit Carow. She remained by Teddy's side until he died.

But soon Teddy was ready for adventure again. In 1895 he became the police commissioner of New York City. He loved to walk the streets with his policemen. He worked long and hard hours to stamp out crime.

But the most exciting time of Teddy's life came during the Spanish-American War, when America went to war against Spain.

Since 1885, Cuban rebels had been fighting against their Spanish rulers. Many Americans demanded that the United States help the Cubans. Cuba is only ninety miles from the coast of Florida. People in the United States were afraid that Spain wanted to invade the United States.

In February of 1898 a United States battleship called the *Maine* blew up. Americans blamed the Spanish. Right away Teddy began looking for men who could fight in the hot Cuban weather. Most of the men he found were college athletes or cowboys. The newspapers called these men "Roosevelt's Rough Riders."

The Rough Riders fought many battles while they were in Cuba. The most famous one was at San Juan Hill. The Rough Riders fought bravely against the Spanish army. They did not wait for other soldiers to help them. On July 1, 1898, the Rough Riders helped take over the Spanish fort on San Juan Hill. They let out a cry that had been yelled around the country—"Remember the *Maine*!" Teddy Roosevelt was once again called "the fearless one!"

The United States army defeated the Spanish and made Cuba a safe place. People in the United States were very happy. They declared Roosevelt and his Rough Riders national heroes.

Later that year New York State needed a new governor. The people elected Teddy Roosevelt because of his part in the Spanish-American War. As governor Teddy said one of his most famous quotes, "Speak softly and carry a big stick, and you will go far!"

Teddy's popularity as governor of New York did carry him far. In 1901 he became vice president of the United States with President William McKinley. Roosevelt could hardly believe he was on his way to the nation's capital.

Chapter 3
A Changing World

Just as Teddy was getting used to life in Washington, D.C., another tragedy struck.

In September of 1901 President McKinley was killed. As vice president, Teddy took President McKinley's place.

It was an amazing time to be president. New inventions were being created. Airplanes, automobiles, and movies were all invented during this time.

Teddy Roosevelt was a popular president. He did many good things for the country. But he was also a great man and a great father.

Perhaps one of the things Teddy Roosevelt is most loved for is his part in the creation of the teddy bear. One of the stories is that when Teddy Roosevelt was traveling in Mississippi in 1902, he saw a bear cub that had been captured and tied to a tree. President Roosevelt untied the cub and let it go free. This was unheard of during a time when hunting bears was a favorite sport.

Morris and Rose Michtom of Brooklyn, New York, made a toy bear to honor the president saving the cub. They put the bear in their shop window. Everyone who saw the stuffed toy wanted one. Soon the "Teddy bear" became a symbol of good deeds and gained the love of children everywhere.

Another famous story about Teddy involved the fun and love he had for his children. Teddy and Edith had five children: Theodore III, Kermit, Ethel, Archibald, and Quentin. Teddy's daughter Alice also lived with them. The children and their friends were called the "White House Gang."

Once the White House Gang sent a
letter to Teddy declaring war on the
United States. Teddy then declared war
on his children. The Gang would pop
up in important meetings. He would
surprise them during their lunch. This
went on for several days until the
president declared himself the winner
and the children were all sent to bed.

Another time the White House Gang
got in trouble because they covered
famous paintings of past presidents
with spitballs.

Even though he had fun with his children, Teddy Roosevelt was known as a tough president. He fought big business. He tried to make life easier for poor people. Most of all, he cared about the wildlife of this great country. Because of him many animals and birds were protected.

Theodore Roosevelt won another term as president from 1905 to 1909. During his second term he continued to fight for what he believed in. Weak little Teddy had become a strong, fearless man.

Here is a time line of Theodore Roosevelt's life:

1858   Born October 27 in New York City

1880   Marries Alice Hathaway Lee on October 27

1882–1884   Served in the New York State Assembly

1884   Alice Roosevelt dies

1886   Marries Edith Kermit Carow in London

1897   Named assistant secretary of the Navy

1898   Leads the "Rough Riders" in the Spanish-American War

1899   Becomes governor of New York State

1900   Elected vice president of the United States under President McKinley

1901   Becomes twenty-sixth president of the United States

1904   Elected to full term as president of the United States

1906   Awarded Nobel Peace Prize

1912   Defeated in presidential election on the "Bull Moose" ticket

1919   Dies at his home in Oyster Bay, New York, on January 6